AGI
Artificial General Intelligence

Krikor Karaoghlanian

To all the future AGI researchers and enthusiasts, may this book ignite your curiosity and inspire you to explore the limitless possibilities of artificial intelligence.

Success in creating effective AI, could be the biggest event in the history of our civilization. Or the worst. We just don't know. So we cannot know if we will be infinitely helped by AI, or ignored by it and side-lined, or conceivably destroyed by it.
Stephen Hawking

CONTENTS

INTRODUCTION

Artificial Intelligence (AI) has come a long way since the concept was first introduced in the mid-twentieth century. Today, we are witnessing an unprecedented acceleration in the development of AI, with applications ranging from self-driving cars and speech recognition to medical diagnosis and personalized marketing. However, despite these impressive achievements, most AI systems are still narrow in their scope and lack the ability to generalize across domains or learn from experience in the way that humans do. This is where Artificial General Intelligence (AGI) comes in.

AGI is a term used to describe the development of machines that can think and learn like humans, possessing the ability to reason, solve problems, and make decisions independently. Unlike narrow AI systems, which are designed to perform specific tasks, AGI seeks to create machines that are capable of understanding the world in the same way that humans do. This has the potential to revolutionize every aspect of our lives, from healthcare and education to transportation and entertainment.

In this book, we explore the exciting and rapidly evolving field of AGI. We begin by providing an overview of the history and current state of AI, including the breakthroughs that have paved the way for AGI. We then delve into the technical and theoretical foundations of AGI, exploring the latest research in machine learning, cognitive psychology, and neuroscience. Along the way, we examine the challenges and ethical implications of developing AGI, and how it could shape the future of humanity.

Whether you are a student, researcher, or simply someone who is interested in the intersection of technology and humanity, this book provides a comprehensive and accessible introduction to one of the most important and exciting topics of our time: AGI.

WHAT IS AGI?

AGI, or Artificial General Intelligence, refers to the development of AI systems that can perform tasks and make decisions in a way that is similar to human intelligence. Unlike narrow AI systems, which are designed to perform specific tasks such as image recognition or language translation, AGI is meant to be more general and versatile, capable of learning and adapting to new situations and tasks in a way that is comparable to how humans do it.

The idea of AGI has been around for decades, but it has only recently become a more realistic goal due to advances in machine learning, neural networks, and other AI technologies. While we are still far from achieving true AGI, researchers and engineers around the world are working on developing the algorithms, hardware, and data infrastructure necessary to make it a reality.

One of the defining characteristics of AGI is its ability to reason, plan, and make decisions in complex and uncertain environments. This requires not only a high degree of computational power, but also a deep understanding of human cognition, including perception, reasoning, and emotion. To achieve this, researchers are exploring a range of techniques, from deep learning and reinforcement learning to Bayesian inference and symbolic reasoning.

Another important aspect of AGI is its potential impact on society and the economy. As AGI systems become more powerful and versatile, they could transform many industries and sectors, from healthcare and transportation to finance and education. This could lead to significant benefits for humanity, such as improved efficiency, better decision-making, and new opportunities for creativity and innovation. However, it could also create new challenges and risks, such as job displacement, economic inequality, and ethical concerns around the use of AI.

Despite these challenges, many researchers and experts believe that AGI could be one of the most transformative technologies of the 21st century, with the potential to shape the future of humanity in profound and unexpected ways. As such, it is an area of research and development that deserves careful attention and consideration from policymakers, industry leaders, and the public at large.

WHY IS AGI AN IMPORTANT TOPIC?

AGI is an important topic because it has the potential to revolutionize every aspect of human life, from the way we work and communicate to the way we solve problems and make decisions. With AGI, machines would be able to understand and interpret complex information, learn and adapt from new experiences, and reason and make decisions based on that knowledge. This would enable them to perform tasks that currently require human intelligence and decision-making abilities.

AGI could also help address some of the world's most pressing problems, such as climate change, disease prevention, and poverty. For example, AGI-powered technologies could be used to optimize energy consumption, develop new treatments for diseases, and improve resource allocation in developing countries. Furthermore, AGI could lead to advances in fields such as robotics, automation, and autonomous vehicles, which could have significant economic and societal impacts.

However, the development of AGI also raises important ethical, social, and economic considerations. As machines become more intelligent and capable, they could potentially replace human workers in many industries, leading to job displacement and economic inequality. AGI could also have unintended consequences, such as the development of autonomous weapons or the loss of privacy.

Therefore, it is crucial that we understand the potential benefits and risks of AGI and carefully consider how to develop and regulate this technology in a way that maximizes its benefits while minimizing its potential negative impacts.

SCOPE OF THE BOOK

Artificial General Intelligence (AGI) is an emerging field of research that aims to develop intelligent machines that can perform a wide range of tasks, similar to the cognitive abilities of human beings. Unlike narrow or specialized AI, which is designed to perform specific tasks, AGI is intended to be a more general form of intelligence that can adapt and learn in a variety of contexts, with the potential to exceed human intelligence in various domains.

The importance of AGI lies in its potential to revolutionize various aspects of human life, including healthcare, transportation, manufacturing, education, and entertainment. AGI can also help address some of the most pressing challenges facing humanity, such as climate change, poverty, and disease. However, AGI also raises significant ethical and social concerns, such as job displacement, privacy infringement, and the risk of autonomous weapons and other forms of AI misuse.

The scope of this book is to provide a comprehensive overview of AGI, including its history, theoretical foundations, technological advancements, ethical and social implications, and potential applications. It covers various topics, such as machine learning, natural language processing, robotics, cognitive architectures, and the future of work and education in the age of AGI.

The book is intended to be accessible to a wide audience, from students and researchers in AI and related fields, to policymakers, educators, and general readers who want to understand the implications of AGI for the future of humanity. The book also provides a critical perspective on the current state of AGI research, the challenges and opportunities it presents, and the possible scenarios for its development and deployment.

OVERVIEW OF THE CONTENTS

The History of AI and AGI
This chapter provides a historical overview of AI research, from its early beginnings to the evolution of AGI. It also discusses the milestones and breakthroughs in AGI development.

The Science of AGI
This chapter delves into the theoretical foundations of AGI and explores various cognitive architectures for AGI, including deep learning, reinforcement learning, natural language processing, computer vision, robotics, and embodied intelligence.

Approaches to AGI
This chapter discusses different approaches to AGI, including symbolic AI, connectionism and neural networks, hybrid approaches, biological inspiration, and neuromorphic computing. It also explores the potential of quantum computing for AGI.

Recent Advances in AGI Research
This chapter provides an overview of the latest AGI platforms, frameworks, algorithms, and techniques, and explores current AGI applications and use cases.

Challenges and Obstacles in AGI Development
This chapter discusses the challenges and obstacles in AGI development, including technical, ethical, and governance issues. It also explores the potential risks and unintended consequences of AGI.

The Benefits of AGI

This chapter explores the potential benefits of AGI, including solving complex problems, positive impact on society and the economy, and improved decision-making and problem-solving.

The Risks of AGI

This chapter explores the potential risks and unintended consequences of AGI, including job displacement, existential risks, bias, and ethical considerations.

Ethics and Governance

This chapter explores the ethical considerations of AGI and the importance of transparency and accountability in its development. It also discusses the role of governments, international organizations, stakeholders, and the public in regulating AGI.

AGI and Society

This chapter explores the social and cultural implications of AGI, its impact on different industries and sectors, and the need for education and workforce development. It also discusses the importance of collaboration and partnerships in the development and deployment of AGI.

The Future of AGI

This chapter explores different scenarios for the future of AGI, its impact on the economy, society, and the environment, and the role of humans in a world with AGI. It also discusses the challenges and opportunities ahead.

Conclusion

This chapter summarizes the key points made in the book, explores the implications for the future of AGI, and provides recommendations for future research and policy development.

THE HISTORY OF AI AND AGI

The history of AI can be traced back to the 1950s, when pioneers such as John McCarthy, Marvin Minsky, and Claude Shannon began exploring the possibility of creating machines that could mimic human intelligence. They envisioned that these machines could perform tasks such as natural language processing, pattern recognition, and logical reasoning. The early years of AI research were marked by significant progress in developing systems that could solve complex problems, such as chess and theorem proving. However, these systems were still limited in their scope and could not match the versatility and flexibility of human intelligence.

In the 1990s, the field of AI experienced a resurgence with the advent of machine learning techniques such as neural networks, decision trees, and support vector machines. These techniques enabled AI systems to learn from large datasets and make predictions and decisions based on patterns and statistical models. This led to the development of applications such as speech recognition, image classification, and recommendation systems.

While the progress in narrow AI was impressive, researchers started to envision a new era of AI that could replicate the versatility and creativity of human intelligence. This led to the emergence of the concept of AGI, which aims to develop machines that can think and reason like humans. Unlike narrow AI, which is designed for specific tasks, AGI is intended to perform a wide range of cognitive functions, such as natural language understanding, common sense reasoning, and problem-solving.

The development of AGI is still in its early stages, and many researchers are exploring different approaches to achieving this goal. Some researchers are focusing on developing hybrid systems that combine rule-based reasoning and machine learning techniques. Others are experimenting with neuromorphic computing, which mimics the structure and function of the human brain. Some are even exploring the possibility of developing conscious machines that can experience emotions and self-awareness.

Despite the challenges and uncertainties surrounding AGI development, there have been significant breakthroughs in recent years. For example, in 2019, OpenAI developed a language model called GPT-2, which demonstrated remarkable natural language processing capabilities. Another notable breakthrough was achieved by DeepMind, which developed AlphaGo, an AI system that beat the world champion in the game of Go, a complex board game with more possible positions than there are atoms in the universe.

In conclusion, the history of AI has been marked by significant progress in developing machines that can perform increasingly complex tasks. The evolution of AGI represents the next frontier of AI research, and it has the potential to revolutionize the world and transform many industries. While there are still many challenges and uncertainties to be addressed, the recent breakthroughs in AGI development provide hope and excitement for the future of AI.

EARLY AI RESEARCH

Early AI research dates back to the mid-20th century, when computer scientists began exploring the concept of artificial intelligence. The term "artificial intelligence" was first coined by John McCarthy in 1955, who is also known for creating the Lisp programming language.

In the late 1950s and early 1960s, researchers developed early AI programs such as the Logic Theorist and the General Problem Solver. These programs were designed to solve specific problems using logical reasoning and search algorithms.

During the 1960s and 1970s, AI research experienced significant growth, thanks in part to the establishment of the Dartmouth Conference in 1956, which is often considered to be the birthplace of AI research. During this time, researchers explored a variety of AI techniques, including rule-based systems, machine learning, and natural language processing.

However, progress in AI research was slow during the 1980s and 1990s due to a lack of funding and limited computing power. It wasn't until the turn of the millennium that AI research began to experience a resurgence, thanks in part to advancements in computing technology and the availability of large amounts of data.

This resurgence in AI research paved the way for the development of AGI, which seeks to create intelligent machines capable of performing a wide range of tasks, rather than being limited to specific applications. The rest of this chapter will explore the milestones and breakthroughs in AGI development.

THE EVOLUTION OF AGI

The evolution of AGI (Artificial General Intelligence) has been a long and challenging process. While AI (Artificial Intelligence) research has been ongoing since the mid-20th century, the focus on developing AGI has gained traction in recent years. AGI is a system that can understand or learn any intellectual task that a human can.

In the early days of AI, researchers focused on developing systems that could perform specific tasks, such as playing chess or recognizing speech. These systems were designed to mimic human intelligence in a narrow sense, but they lacked the broader abilities of human beings.

However, in the 21st century, the field of AI research shifted its focus towards developing AGI. This shift in focus has been driven by the recognition that narrow AI systems have limitations and cannot solve complex problems that require a more holistic approach.

The development of AGI requires a deeper understanding of human intelligence and the ability to replicate it in machines. This has led to the emergence of new fields of research, such as cognitive science and neuroscience, which are focused on understanding the human brain and how it processes information.

AGI research is interdisciplinary, drawing on expertise from fields such as computer science, psychology, philosophy, and mathematics. The ultimate goal is to develop a system that can learn and adapt to any situation, in the same way that humans can.

Despite the progress that has been made in AGI research, there are still significant challenges that need to be overcome. These include developing algorithms that can learn from experience, understanding how to represent and manipulate complex knowledge, and creating systems that can reason and make decisions based on incomplete information.

Nonetheless, the development of AGI has the potential to revolutionize many industries and improve our daily lives in countless ways. It is an exciting and rapidly evolving field that will undoubtedly continue to shape our future.

MILESTONES AND BREAKTHROUGHS IN AGI DEVELOPMENT

The development of AGI has been a gradual process, marked by several important milestones and breakthroughs. Some of the most significant ones are:

1.Turing Test: In 1950, British mathematician and computer scientist Alan Turing proposed the Turing Test, a measure of a machine's ability to exhibit intelligent behavior that is indistinguishable from that of a human. Although the test has been heavily criticized, it remains a landmark in the field of AI research.

2.Expert Systems: In the 1970s and 80s, expert systems emerged as a new approach to AI. These systems were designed to mimic the decision-making abilities of human experts in specific domains, such as medical diagnosis or financial analysis.

3.Neural Networks: In the 1980s, neural networks became an important tool in AI research. These networks were modeled after the structure of the human brain and were capable of learning and adapting to new information.

4. Learning: In the early 2010s, deep learning emerged as a breakthrough in AI research. This approach to machine learning uses large neural networks with many layers to learn from vast amounts of data, allowing machines to recognize patterns and make predictions with unprecedented accuracy.

5.Reinforcement Learning: Another important breakthrough in AGI development is reinforcement learning. This approach involves teaching machines through trial and error, allowing them to learn from their mistakes and improve their performance over time.

6.OpenAI's GPT-3: In 2020, OpenAI released the GPT-3 language model, which represents a significant step towards AGI. With 175 billion parameters, GPT-3 is one of the largest and most powerful language models ever created, capable of performing a wide range of language tasks with remarkable accuracy.

THE SCIENCE OF AGI

Artificial General Intelligence (AGI) is a field of study that aims to create intelligent machines that can perform a wide range of tasks similar to humans. This chapter explores the theoretical foundations of AGI and the various cognitive architectures used to achieve it.

One of the main challenges in developing AGI is creating an intelligent system that can adapt and learn from new experiences. This has led to the development of various cognitive architectures, which provide a framework for organizing and understanding the different components of an intelligent system.

Deep learning is a popular cognitive architecture used in AGI research. It involves training artificial neural networks to learn from large datasets and make accurate predictions. Reinforcement learning is another approach, which involves an agent learning through trial and error to maximize rewards in a given environment.

Natural language processing (NLP) is a subfield of AI that focuses on enabling machines to understand, interpret, and generate human language. NLP plays a critical role in developing AGI systems that can communicate effectively with humans.

Computer vision is another essential component of AGI, enabling machines to interpret and analyze visual data. Robotics and embodied intelligence, which involve creating machines that can interact with their physical environment, are also important areas of research in AGI.

This chapter also discusses the challenges and limitations of current AGI research and explores possible future directions for the field. Despite the progress made, there is still a long way to go before we can achieve true AGI.

In summary, this chapter provides a comprehensive overview of the theoretical foundations and cognitive architectures used in AGI research. Understanding these components is critical in developing intelligent machines that can perform tasks similar to humans.

THEORETICAL FOUNDATIONS OF AGI

The theoretical foundations of AGI are rooted in cognitive science and artificial intelligence research. AGI aims to develop machines that can perform a wide range of tasks with human-level intelligence and flexibility. This requires a theoretical understanding of how human cognition works and how it can be replicated in machines.

One of the key theoretical foundations of AGI is the idea of general intelligence. General intelligence refers to the ability to learn, reason, and solve problems in a broad range of domains, rather than being specialized in a narrow area. The concept of general intelligence is based on the idea that there is a fundamental cognitive architecture that underlies all intelligent behavior.

Another important theoretical foundation of AGI is the concept of embodied cognition. Embodied cognition is the idea that cognitive processes are closely tied to physical embodiment and the environment in which an agent is situated. This means that an AGI system needs to be able to interact with the physical world and perceive and manipulate objects in order to develop a robust and flexible understanding of the world.

Additionally, theories of consciousness and self-awareness are also important in the development of AGI. These theories explore the nature of subjective experience and how it can be replicated in machines.

Overall, a strong theoretical foundation is essential for the development of AGI, as it provides the framework for building intelligent systems that can learn, reason, and interact with the world in a way that is similar to human intelligence.

COGNITIVE ARCHITECTURES FOR AGI

AGI researchers have explored various cognitive architectures as potential candidates for achieving AGI. These architectures are models of how the mind works, and they aim to provide a framework for building intelligent machines that can reason, learn, and adapt like humans.

One of the most prominent cognitive architectures for AGI is the Soar architecture, which is based on the idea of problem-solving and decision-making. Soar combines rule-based reasoning, cognitive modeling, and reinforcement learning to provide a general-purpose cognitive architecture for intelligent agents.

Another widely used cognitive architecture for AGI is the ACT-R architecture, which focuses on human cognitive performance and uses a combination of declarative and procedural knowledge to model cognition. ACT-R has been applied to a wide range of cognitive tasks, including language processing, memory, problem-solving, and decision-making.

Other cognitive architectures for AGI include the Global Workspace Theory, which proposes that consciousness arises from the interaction between different cognitive modules, and the Neural Engineering Framework, which uses neural models to build intelligent systems that can learn and adapt to their environment.

Each of these cognitive architectures has its own strengths and limitations, and the choice of architecture depends on the specific application and requirements of the AGI system. Researchers continue to explore new cognitive architectures and refine existing ones in the quest for AGI.

DEEP LEARNING AND NEURAL NETWORKS

Deep learning and neural networks are one of the most popular approaches used in developing AGI. Deep learning is a type of machine learning that uses artificial neural networks to learn and recognize patterns in data. These networks are designed to simulate the behavior of the human brain by creating multiple layers of nodes that process information and learn from it. Deep learning has been successful in achieving human-like performance in tasks such as image recognition, natural language processing, and speech recognition.

Neural networks are the backbone of deep learning and have been around since the 1940s. They are computational models that are designed to simulate the behavior of neurons in the brain. Neural networks consist of layers of nodes, each of which performs a specific operation on the input data. The output of one layer becomes the input to the next layer, and so on until the final output is produced.

Deep learning and neural networks have revolutionized the field of AI, enabling significant breakthroughs in AGI development. These techniques have the potential to unlock the full capabilities of AGI by allowing machines to learn and adapt to new situations in a way that was previously impossible.

REINFORCEMENT LEARNING

Reinforcement learning is a type of machine learning where an agent learns to make decisions by interacting with an environment. The agent receives feedback in the form of rewards or penalties based on its actions, and the goal is to maximize the total reward over time. Reinforcement learning has been successfully applied to a variety of problems, including game playing, robotics, and autonomous driving. One of the key advantages of reinforcement learning is its ability to handle complex, dynamic environments where the optimal strategy may change over time.

However, there are also some challenges associated with reinforcement learning. One of the main challenges is the need for large amounts of data and computational resources, which can make it difficult to apply reinforcement learning to real-world problems. Another challenge is the issue of exploration versus exploitation, where the agent must balance between trying out new actions to learn more about the environment and exploiting its current knowledge to maximize rewards. Researchers continue to explore new techniques and algorithms to address these challenges and improve the performance of reinforcement learning in AGI systems.

NATURAL LANGUAGE PROCESSING AND UNDERSTANDING

Natural language processing (NLP) is a branch of AI that deals with the interaction between computers and humans using natural language. The goal of NLP is to enable machines to understand, interpret, and generate human language. NLP has been an important area of research in AGI due to the critical role of language in human cognition and communication.

One of the early breakthroughs in NLP was the development of the first machine translation system in the 1950s. Since then, NLP has made significant progress in various areas such as speech recognition, sentiment analysis, and question-answering systems. With the advent of deep learning, NLP has witnessed a remarkable improvement in performance, leading to the development of several state-of-the-art models such as BERT, GPT, and T5.

One of the challenges in NLP is dealing with the ambiguity and complexity of natural language. Human language is highly context-dependent, and words can have multiple meanings depending on the context in which they are used. To address this challenge, NLP models use sophisticated algorithms such as transformers and attention mechanisms to capture the contextual information and disambiguate the meaning of words.

NLP has numerous applications in AGI, including virtual assistants, chatbots, and personalization systems. The ability to understand and generate human language is critical for AGI to interact with humans in a natural and meaningful way.

COMPUTER VISION

Computer vision is another critical component in developing AGI. The ability to perceive, interpret and understand visual information is crucial for creating intelligent machines capable of interacting with the physical world. Computer vision enables machines to recognize and identify objects, people, and other visual cues in real-time, just like humans.

One of the most significant advancements in computer vision is the use of deep convolutional neural networks (CNNs). These networks can learn to recognize and classify images by using hierarchical layers of neurons that progressively extract more complex features from the visual data. CNNs have revolutionized computer vision applications, such as image and video recognition, face detection, and object tracking.

Another critical aspect of computer vision in AGI is 3D perception. While humans can perceive the world in 3D and interact with it effortlessly, replicating this capability in machines has been challenging. However, recent advancements in depth sensing technologies, such as LiDAR and stereo cameras, have made it possible for machines to perceive depth and create 3D models of the environment. This capability is essential for robotics and autonomous vehicles, enabling them to navigate and interact with the world around them.

ROBOTICS AND EMBODIED INTELLIGENCE

Robotics is an important field for developing AGI, as robots can interact with the physical world and gain knowledge from sensory data. Embodied intelligence is the concept of integrating intelligence with the body and environment, allowing AGI to adapt and learn from experiences.

One of the challenges of robotics and embodied intelligence is designing systems that can perceive, reason, and act in a way that is consistent with human intuition and expectations. For example, robots should be able to understand social cues and norms, such as avoiding invading personal space or respecting hierarchy.

There are various approaches to robotics and embodied intelligence, such as behavior-based robotics, which focuses on generating complex behavior through the interaction of simple behaviors, and developmental robotics, which models the cognitive development of humans and animals to create intelligent robots. Additionally, there is research on integrating AI with the brain and nervous system to create brain-computer interfaces and neuromorphic computing.

APPROACHES TO AGI

This chapter discusses various approaches to achieving AGI and the potential benefits and drawbacks of each approach. It covers symbolic AI, connectionism and neural networks, hybrid approaches, biological inspiration, and neuromorphic computing, as well as the potential of quantum computing for AGI.

Symbolic AI involves the use of logical rules and knowledge representation to solve problems, while connectionism and neural networks are based on the concept of distributed processing and pattern recognition. Hybrid approaches combine these two approaches for a more comprehensive approach to AGI.

Biological inspiration involves studying the structure and function of the brain to understand how intelligence works and how it can be replicated in machines. Neuromorphic computing is a recent development that involves creating computer chips that function like the human brain.

Finally, this chapter explores the potential of quantum computing for AGI. Quantum computing offers a new approach to computing that may provide the necessary processing power for AGI.

Overall, this chapter provides a comprehensive overview of the different approaches to achieving AGI and highlights the potential benefits and limitations of each approach.

SYMBOLIC AI

Symbolic AI, also known as rule-based AI, is based on the idea of representing knowledge and reasoning through logical rules and symbols. In this approach, an AI system consists of a set of rules that can be used to infer new knowledge from existing knowledge. The rules are expressed in a formal language, such as first-order logic or predicate calculus, and the system uses algorithms to manipulate the rules to perform reasoning.

One of the main advantages of symbolic AI is that it allows for transparent and interpretable reasoning, as the rules can be examined and understood by human experts. It is also well-suited for applications where logical reasoning and knowledge representation are important, such as expert systems, natural language processing, and planning.

However, symbolic AI has some limitations, particularly in dealing with uncertainty and complex real-world problems. In many cases, it requires a large knowledge base and may struggle with problems that do not have clear rules or require reasoning about probabilities and uncertainties. As a result, researchers have explored alternative approaches to AGI that seek to overcome these limitations.

CONNECTIONISM AND NEURAL NETWORKS

Connectionism and neural networks, also known as parallel distributed processing (PDP), is another approach to AGI that has gained significant attention in recent years. It is inspired by the structure and function of the human brain, and it models cognition as the result of the interaction of simple processing units (neurons) that are connected to each other in complex ways.

Neural networks have shown significant success in pattern recognition tasks, such as image and speech recognition, and natural language processing. They are also used in reinforcement learning algorithms, where an agent learns to perform tasks through trial-and-error interactions with the environment.

One of the main advantages of neural networks is their ability to learn from data and generalize to new, unseen examples. This makes them highly useful in situations where the underlying rules or patterns are not well understood or difficult to express in a symbolic form.

However, neural networks also have their limitations. They can be computationally expensive, require large amounts of data for training, and can be prone to overfitting, where the model fits the training data too well and performs poorly on new, unseen data.

HYBRID APPROACHES

Hybrid approaches refer to the integration of multiple AI techniques to achieve AGI. For example, a hybrid approach could combine symbolic AI with deep learning to create a more robust and flexible system. Another hybrid approach could combine reinforcement learning with computer vision to develop an AI system that can learn from visual input and take actions based on the learned information. Hybrid approaches offer a way to overcome the limitations of individual techniques and create more comprehensive and adaptable AGI systems. However, developing effective hybrid approaches requires a deep understanding of the strengths and weaknesses of each technique and how they can be combined effectively.

Hybrid approaches combine multiple techniques and architectures to create more robust and flexible AGI systems. For example, a hybrid approach could involve combining symbolic AI with connectionism to leverage the strengths of both approaches. This can lead to improved performance and the ability to handle more complex tasks.

Another example of a hybrid approach is the combination of deep learning and reinforcement learning. Deep learning is used to extract high-level features from raw input data, while reinforcement learning is used to train agents to perform specific tasks through trial and error. This approach has been successfully applied in various domains, including game playing, robotics, and autonomous driving.

One of the key advantages of hybrid approaches is their ability to overcome the limitations of individual approaches. For example, while symbolic AI is good at reasoning and logic, it often struggles with handling uncertain or incomplete information. On the other hand, connectionism and neural networks excel at pattern recognition and processing large amounts of data, but they may lack the ability to perform high-level reasoning. By combining these approaches, hybrid AGI systems can leverage the strengths of each component to overcome their weaknesses.

However, developing hybrid AGI systems can be challenging due to the complexity and heterogeneity of the components involved. Integrating different architectures and techniques requires careful design and engineering to ensure that the system is coherent and effective. Despite the challenges, hybrid approaches represent a promising direction for AGI research and are likely to play a significant role in the development of intelligent machines in the future.

BIOLOGICAL INSPIRATION AND NEUROMORPHIC COMPUTING

Biological inspiration refers to the approach of modeling AGI after biological systems, such as the brain. The goal is to replicate the structure and function of biological neurons and synapses to create artificial neural networks. This approach has led to the development of neuromorphic computing, which is a type of computing that mimics the behavior of biological systems. Neuromorphic computing systems are designed to process information using patterns and connections, similar to the way the brain works.

One of the advantages of neuromorphic computing is its ability to perform tasks quickly and efficiently, using less power than traditional computing systems. This makes it an attractive approach for AGI development, especially for applications that require real-time processing or low power consumption.

However, one of the challenges of neuromorphic computing is its complexity. The brain is a highly complex system, and replicating its function in an artificial system is a daunting task. Additionally, there are limitations in our understanding of the brain and how it works, which presents obstacles for AGI researchers using this approach.

Despite these challenges, there have been notable breakthroughs in neuromorphic computing, including the development of neuromorphic chips that can simulate the behavior of neurons and synapses. As research in this field continues, it holds great promise for the future of AGI development.

QUANTUM COMPUTING AND AGI

Quantum computing is a relatively new technology that has the potential to revolutionize AGI research. Unlike classical computers, which use bits to store and process information, quantum computers use quantum bits or qubits, which can exist in multiple states at once. This property allows quantum computers to perform certain types of calculations much faster than classical computers, making them ideal for certain AGI applications.

One of the key challenges in AGI research is dealing with the massive amounts of data involved in training and testing intelligent systems. Quantum computers could potentially help overcome this challenge by enabling faster and more efficient processing of large data sets.

Another potential application of quantum computing in AGI is in the development of quantum neural networks, which could be used to model complex biological systems more accurately than classical neural networks.

Despite the promise of quantum computing, there are still many technical and practical challenges that must be overcome before it can be fully integrated into AGI research. Nonetheless, many experts believe that quantum computing has the potential to unlock new breakthroughs in AGI development in the years to come.

RECENT ADVANCES IN AGI RESEARCH

In this chapter, we explore the latest advancements in AGI research, including platforms, frameworks, algorithms, and techniques. We also take a closer look at current applications and use cases for AGI.

One of the recent breakthroughs in AGI research is the development of OpenAI's GPT-3, a powerful language model that can understand and generate human-like text. GPT-3 has shown impressive performance in various natural language processing tasks, including language translation, summarization, and question answering.

Another notable advancement in AGI research is the emergence of reinforcement learning techniques for robotics. Researchers have been able to train robots to perform complex tasks in dynamic environments using reinforcement learning algorithms, which allow the robots to learn from their mistakes and improve their performance over time.

In addition to these advancements, there are also ongoing efforts to develop AGI platforms and frameworks that can be easily customized and integrated into different applications. For example, Google's TensorFlow and Facebook's PyTorch are popular open-source frameworks for building and training machine learning models, including AGI models.

Overall, recent advancements in AGI research have opened up new possibilities for intelligent machines that can perform complex tasks and adapt to different environments. The applications of AGI are vast and wide-ranging, from autonomous vehicles and healthcare to finance and education. Understanding these advancements and their potential is critical for shaping the future of intelligent machines.

AGI PLATFORMS AND FRAMEWORKS

AGI platforms and frameworks refer to software tools and libraries that provide a foundation for AGI development. These platforms typically offer a range of features such as data management, algorithm development, training and testing models, and deployment of trained models.

Some of the popular AGI platforms and frameworks include OpenAI, Google's TensorFlow, Microsoft's Cognitive Toolkit, PyTorch, and Caffe. Each of these platforms has its strengths and weaknesses, depending on the specific use case and application.

OpenAI, for example, provides a comprehensive suite of AGI tools and technologies, including language processing, computer vision, and robotics. It also has a range of applications, including chatbots, image recognition, and language translation.

TensorFlow, on the other hand, is a popular open-source framework for machine learning that provides robust support for deep learning and neural networks. It offers a range of features such as data preprocessing, model building, training, and deployment, and has been used for various applications such as image and speech recognition, language processing, and anomaly detection.

PyTorch is another open-source machine learning framework that is popular among researchers and developers. It provides a flexible and intuitive interface for building and training models, and is well-suited for deep learning and natural language processing applications.

Overall, these AGI platforms and frameworks are critical

components in advancing AGI research and development, as they provide a foundation for building intelligent systems and applications.

NEW ALGORITHMS AND TECHNIQUES

Recent advances in AGI research have led to the development of new algorithms and techniques that have significantly improved the performance of AGI systems. One such technique is transfer learning, which allows AGI systems to leverage knowledge gained from one task to perform another related task more efficiently.

Another technique that has gained popularity in recent years is generative adversarial networks (GANs), which are deep neural networks that can generate synthetic data that is almost indistinguishable from real data. This technique has applications in fields such as computer vision and natural language processing, where it can be used to generate realistic images or text.

Other recent advances in AGI research include the development of new optimization algorithms, such as the adaptive moment estimation (Adam) algorithm, and the use of reinforcement learning to train AGI systems to learn from their own experience, much like humans do.

These new algorithms and techniques have led to significant improvements in AGI performance, making it possible to tackle more complex and challenging problems. As AGI research continues to advance, we can expect to see even more innovative algorithms and techniques that push the boundaries of what is possible with intelligent machines.

AGI APPLICATIONS AND USE CASES

There are numerous applications and use cases of AGI, ranging from industries like healthcare, finance, and manufacturing to scientific research and exploration. Here are some examples of how AGI is being used:

Healthcare: AGI is being used in the healthcare industry to develop personalized medicine and drug discovery. It is also being used to analyze medical data, such as medical images and patient records, to improve diagnoses and treatments.

Finance: AGI is being used in the finance industry to develop predictive models for market trends and fraud detection. It is also being used for risk analysis and investment management.

Manufacturing: AGI is being used in the manufacturing industry to improve efficiency and productivity. It is being used to optimize supply chain management, quality control, and predictive maintenance.

Scientific research and exploration: AGI is being used in scientific research and exploration to analyze large data sets and to develop simulations and models for complex systems, such as climate models and particle physics.

Robotics and automation: AGI is being used in robotics and automation to develop intelligent robots and autonomous systems for various applications, such as agriculture, logistics, and space exploration.

Personal assistants: AGI can be used to create virtual personal assistants that can understand natural language, anticipate user needs, and carry out tasks on their behalf.

Medical diagnosis and treatment: AGI can be used to analyze patient data and medical images to assist doctors in diagnosing and treating diseases.

Autonomous vehicles: AGI can be used to develop autonomous vehicles that can navigate complex environments, recognize objects, and make decisions in real-time.

Manufacturing: AGI can be used to optimize manufacturing processes, reduce waste, and increase efficiency.

Finance: AGI can be used in financial applications such as fraud detection, risk assessment, and portfolio optimization.

Education: AGI can be used to develop intelligent tutoring systems that can adapt to the needs of individual learners and provide personalized instruction.

Gaming: AGI can be used to create more advanced and realistic game environments, as well as to develop non-player characters with more sophisticated behaviors and decision-making abilities.

Natural language processing: AGI can be used to improve natural language processing capabilities, allowing machines to better understand and respond to human language.

Space exploration: AGI can be used to develop autonomous spacecraft that can navigate and explore other planets.

Agriculture: AGI can be used to optimize farming practices, improve crop yields, and reduce waste.

CHALLENGES AND OBSTACLES IN AGI DEVELOPMENT

AGI development faces several challenges and obstacles that must be overcome to achieve the goal of building truly intelligent machines.

One major challenge is the lack of a unified theory of intelligence. Despite significant progress in understanding the cognitive processes involved in intelligence, there is no agreed-upon definition or framework that can guide AGI research.

Another challenge is the difficulty of integrating multiple cognitive functions and modalities into a cohesive system. Current AGI systems often excel in specific tasks, such as natural language processing or image recognition, but struggle to integrate these abilities into a broader context of understanding and decision-making.

AGI development also faces technical challenges related to scalability, adaptability, and robustness. As AGI systems become more complex, they must be able to learn and adapt to new situations, generalize from limited data, and handle unpredictable environments and inputs.

Moreover, ethical and social considerations must be addressed to ensure that AGI is developed and deployed in a responsible and beneficial way. This includes issues such as bias, privacy, security, and the potential impact of AGI on employment and society as a whole.

Finally, the development of AGI requires significant investment and collaboration across multiple disciplines, including computer science, neuroscience, psychology, and philosophy. Cooperation and coordination among researchers, institutions, and governments will be critical in making progress toward the goal of AGI.

THE BENEFITS OF AGI

Artificial General Intelligence (AGI) has the potential to provide numerous benefits to society, ranging from solving complex problems to improving decision-making and problem-solving. In this chapter, we explore the potential benefits of AGI in detail.

Solving Complex Problems: AGI has the potential to solve complex problems that are currently beyond human capabilities. For example, AGI could be used to design new materials for energy storage, or to optimize complex logistics networks for maximum efficiency.

Positive Impact on Society and the Economy: AGI has the potential to drive economic growth by improving productivity and efficiency. It could also help solve some of the world's most pressing social and environmental problems, such as climate change, food security, and healthcare.

Improved Decision-Making and Problem-Solving: AGI can help humans make better decisions and solve problems more efficiently by providing insights and recommendations based on vast amounts of data. For example, it could help doctors diagnose and treat diseases more accurately, or help financial analysts make better investment decisions.

Improved Human-Machine Interaction: AGI can improve human-machine interaction by enabling machines to understand and interpret human behavior and language. This could lead to more natural and intuitive interfaces for humans to interact with machines.

Despite the potential benefits, AGI also poses significant risks and challenges. These risks include the potential for misuse or abuse of the technology, as well as the possibility of unintended consequences. It is therefore essential that AGI research and development are guided by ethical principles and are subject to appropriate governance and oversight.

In conclusion, AGI has the potential to provide numerous benefits to society, from solving complex problems to improving decision-making and problem-solving. However, it is essential to approach AGI development with caution and responsibility to ensure that the risks and challenges are adequately addressed.

HOW AGI CAN HELP SOLVE COMPLEX PROBLEMS

AGI has the potential to help solve complex problems in various fields, such as healthcare, climate change, and transportation. For example, in healthcare, AGI can be used to analyze vast amounts of medical data and help physicians make more accurate diagnoses and treatment plans. It can also assist in drug discovery by identifying new drug candidates and predicting their efficacy and side effects.

In the field of climate change, AGI can help analyze data from satellites, sensors, and other sources to monitor and model climate patterns and predict natural disasters. It can also aid in developing sustainable solutions, such as renewable energy technologies and energy-efficient infrastructure.

In transportation, AGI can improve traffic flow and reduce congestion by analyzing traffic patterns and providing real-time recommendations for drivers. It can also assist in developing autonomous vehicles that can increase safety and reduce accidents.

Overall, the potential applications of AGI in solving complex problems are vast and varied, and the technology has the potential to revolutionize various fields and make significant contributions to human progress.

POTENTIAL APPLICATIONS OF AGI IN VARIOUS FIELDS

AGI has the potential to revolutionize various fields by providing new and innovative solutions to long-standing problems. Here are some potential applications of AGI in different fields:

Healthcare: AGI can aid in the development of personalized medicine and provide more accurate and timely diagnoses. It can also be used to analyze large amounts of medical data and identify patterns and correlations that may not be visible to humans.

Agriculture: AGI can help optimize crop yields by providing insights into soil conditions, weather patterns, and crop health. It can also be used to develop new and more efficient farming methods.

Finance: AGI can aid in financial forecasting and risk management by analyzing large amounts of data and identifying patterns and trends. It can also be used to detect fraud and money laundering.

Manufacturing: AGI can help optimize production processes by analyzing data from sensors and other sources to identify bottlenecks and inefficiencies. It can also be used to improve quality control and reduce waste.

Transportation: AGI can aid in the development of autonomous vehicles and improve traffic flow by analyzing data from sensors and other sources. It can also be used to optimize logistics and supply chain management.

Education: AGI can personalize learning experiences for individual students by analyzing their strengths and weaknesses and providing tailored recommendations. It can also be used to automate grading and provide real-time feedback to teachers and students.

Overall, AGI has the potential to transform various fields and improve the quality of life for people around the world.

POSITIVE IMPACT ON SOCIETY AND THE ECONOMY

AGI has the potential to bring about a significant positive impact on society and the economy. One of the primary benefits of AGI is that it can automate tasks that are currently performed by humans, such as data entry, customer service, and manufacturing. This can free up humans to focus on more creative and complex tasks, ultimately leading to increased productivity and economic growth.

Moreover, AGI can be used in various industries to enhance efficiency and productivity, such as healthcare, transportation, and finance. In healthcare, AGI can help in diagnosing diseases and developing personalized treatment plans for patients. In transportation, AGI can be used to optimize traffic flow and reduce accidents. In finance, AGI can help in predicting market trends and identifying investment opportunities.

AGI can also have a significant impact on education, as it can personalize learning experiences for students and provide more efficient and effective teaching methods. Additionally, AGI can be used for scientific research, as it can analyze large amounts of data and help in making significant discoveries.

Overall, the positive impact of AGI on society and the economy can be far-reaching, as it can lead to increased productivity, efficiency, and innovation in various fields.

IMPROVED DECISION-MAKING AND PROBLEM-SOLVING

AGI has the potential to significantly improve decision-making and problem-solving in various industries and domains. With the ability to analyze large amounts of data, identify patterns and correlations, and make predictions based on past experiences, AGI can help humans make better decisions in complex and uncertain environments.

For example, in healthcare, AGI can help medical professionals in diagnosing diseases and recommending treatment plans based on patient data and medical research. In finance, AGI can be used to predict market trends, optimize investment portfolios, and detect fraud. In manufacturing, AGI can optimize production processes, minimize waste, and improve quality control. In transportation, AGI can help autonomous vehicles navigate complex environments and make split-second decisions to avoid accidents.

AGI can also assist in decision-making and problem-solving in areas such as education, energy, environmental management, and public policy. By providing insights and recommendations based on data analysis, AGI can help humans make informed decisions that benefit individuals, communities, and society as a whole.

Overall, AGI has the potential to revolutionize decision-making and problem-solving across various industries and domains, leading to more efficient and effective outcomes.

THE RISKS OF AGI

While AGI has the potential to bring about significant benefits, it also poses a number of risks and challenges. In this chapter, we will explore some of the key risks associated with AGI, including job displacement, existential risks, bias, and ethical considerations.

Job Displacement:

One of the most immediate concerns with the development of AGI is the potential for job displacement. As intelligent machines become capable of performing a wider range of tasks, there is a risk that many jobs will become automated, leading to unemployment and economic disruption. This is a significant risk, especially in industries where automation is already well-established, such as manufacturing and transportation.

Existential Risks:

Another potential risk of AGI is the possibility of existential risks. As machines become increasingly intelligent, there is a risk that they may pose a threat to human existence, either intentionally or unintentionally. For example, if an AGI system were to become out of control or be programmed with goals that conflict with human values, it could potentially cause harm on a global scale.

Bias:

AGI systems are only as good as the data they are trained on, and there is a risk that biased data could lead to biased outcomes. This is a particular concern in areas such as criminal justice, where algorithms are being used to make decisions about sentencing and parole. If these algorithms are trained on biased data, they could perpetuate existing social inequalities.

Ethical Considerations:

Finally, there are a number of ethical considerations associated with the development and use of AGI. These include issues around transparency, accountability, and privacy. It is important to ensure that AGI systems are designed and used in a way that is transparent, and that individuals have some level of control over how their personal data is used.

In summary, while AGI has the potential to bring about significant benefits, it also poses a number of risks and challenges. It is important to carefully consider these risks and work to mitigate them as much as possible, in order to ensure that AGI is developed and used in a way that is safe, ethical, and beneficial for all.

POTENTIAL UNINTENDED CONSEQUENCES OF AGI

As with any new technology, AGI carries the risk of unintended consequences. One potential consequence is job displacement, as machines become more capable of performing tasks that were once done by humans. This could lead to widespread unemployment and economic disruption.

Another significant risk is the potential for existential threats, such as the development of AGI that could cause harm to humans or the environment. This could occur due to a lack of understanding or control over the system, or as a result of intentional misuse.

Bias is another issue that could arise with AGI, as the algorithms and data sets used to train them may reflect societal biases and perpetuate discrimination. This could have serious ethical implications, such as perpetuating social inequalities or violating individuals' rights.

Furthermore, AGI raises ethical considerations around issues such as accountability, transparency, and control. If AGI systems are developed and deployed without proper safeguards and ethical guidelines, it could lead to unforeseen consequences and negative impacts on society.
It is essential to take these risks seriously and carefully consider the ethical implications of AGI development to ensure that the benefits of AGI are maximized while minimizing its potential harms.

JOB DISPLACEMENT AND ECONOMIC DISRUPTION

The development of AGI is likely to have a significant impact on the job market, potentially leading to widespread job displacement and economic disruption. As machines become increasingly intelligent and capable of performing a wider range of tasks, many jobs that were previously performed by humans may become obsolete. This could result in a significant decrease in demand for certain types of labor, leading to unemployment and economic inequality.

Furthermore, the rise of AGI could also lead to increased concentration of wealth and power in the hands of those who control the technology, exacerbating existing socioeconomic inequalities. There is a risk that the benefits of AGI will accrue primarily to a small group of individuals or corporations, while the negative consequences are borne by society as a whole.

It is essential that policymakers and researchers consider the potential economic implications of AGI and work to mitigate the negative consequences. This may involve developing new education and training programs to help workers transition to new types of employment, implementing policies to redistribute wealth and reduce inequality, and fostering innovation and entrepreneurship in new industries that emerge as a result of AGI.

EXISTENTIAL RISKS AND OTHER POTENTIAL DANGERS

AGI also poses potential existential risks and other dangers. As machines become more intelligent and capable, they may begin to operate outside of human control or understanding. This could lead to unintended consequences, such as the development of AGI systems that are programmed to pursue goals that conflict with human values or interests.

Furthermore, AGI systems could be vulnerable to cyber attacks and manipulation, which could have devastating consequences if used for malicious purposes. There is also the risk of AGI systems being used to develop autonomous weapons or other dangerous technologies, leading to potential escalation of conflicts and human suffering.

Finally, the development of AGI raises ethical concerns about the treatment and rights of intelligent machines. As these machines become more advanced and human-like, questions arise about how they should be treated and what responsibilities we have toward them. It is important to consider these risks and ethical considerations as we continue to develop AGI, in order to mitigate potential negative consequences and ensure that AGI is used in a safe and responsible manner.

BIAS AND ETHICAL CONSIDERATIONS

AGI systems are trained on large datasets that are often biased due to historical and societal factors. This can result in AI systems reproducing and even amplifying existing biases and discrimination, leading to unfair outcomes for certain groups of people. For example, facial recognition software has been found to be less accurate for people with darker skin tones, and language models have been shown to exhibit gender and racial biases in their generated text.

Another ethical concern related to AGI is the potential misuse of the technology by individuals or organizations with malicious intent. AGI systems could be used for cyber attacks, social engineering, or even physical attacks if they are designed and controlled by bad actors. This could pose a significant threat to national security and public safety.

To address these challenges, it is important to develop ethical guidelines and regulations for the development and deployment of AGI systems. These guidelines should prioritize fairness, accountability, transparency, and the protection of individual rights and privacy. It is also important to involve diverse stakeholders, including ethicists, social scientists, and members of the public, in the development and implementation of these guidelines.

ETHICS AND GOVERNANCE

AGI has the potential to bring about significant benefits to society, but it also poses significant ethical challenges. For instance, AGI systems may be programmed to prioritize certain goals over others, which could result in unintended consequences that could be harmful to individuals and society as a whole. Additionally, there is a risk that AGI systems may be biased, perpetuating existing societal inequalities.

To ensure that AGI is developed in a responsible and ethical manner, it is important to establish clear ethical guidelines and principles for its development and use. Transparency and accountability are also critical, and stakeholders must be engaged in the development and governance of AGI systems.

Governments, international organizations, and other stakeholders have an important role to play in regulating AGI. Some have called for the establishment of international regulations and treaties to ensure that AGI is developed and used in a responsible manner. Others have argued that governments should take a more proactive role in funding research and development of AGI, to ensure that the benefits of AGI are shared equitably across society.

Ultimately, it will be up to all of us – as individuals, organizations, and society as a whole – to determine the future of AGI and its impact on humanity. By working together, we can ensure that AGI is developed and used in a way that benefits us all.

THE ETHICAL CONSIDERATIONS OF AGI

The development and deployment of AGI raises a number of ethical considerations, including issues related to privacy, autonomy, responsibility, and the potential for harm to individuals and society as a whole. One major concern is the risk of creating AGI that could become uncontrollable or unpredictable, posing a significant threat to human safety and security. Other ethical issues relate to the potential misuse of AGI, including its use in military applications or in the development of autonomous weapons systems.

Another ethical consideration is the potential for AGI to exacerbate existing social and economic inequalities. As AGI systems become more capable, there is a risk that they could displace human workers in a range of industries, leading to significant job losses and economic disruption. This could lead to a concentration of wealth and power in the hands of a few, exacerbating existing inequalities and undermining social cohesion.

There is also a risk that AGI could be used to perpetuate biases and discrimination in society. If AGI systems are trained on biased data, they may learn and perpetuate those biases, leading to unfair and discriminatory outcomes. This could have significant implications for marginalized and vulnerable communities, exacerbating existing inequalities and social injustices.

Overall, there is a need for careful ethical consideration of the development and deployment of AGI. It is important that these technologies are developed and used in a way that promotes human well-being, while also ensuring that the potential risks and unintended consequences are carefully considered and managed. This requires a multi-stakeholder approach, involving governments, international organizations, researchers, developers, and the public, in order to ensure that AGI is developed and deployed in a responsible and ethical manner.

THE IMPORTANCE OF TRANSPARENCY AND ACCOUNTABILITY

As AGI becomes more advanced and capable of making decisions that have a significant impact on society and individuals, the importance of transparency and accountability in its development becomes crucial. This means that the development process should be open and transparent, and stakeholders should have access to information on how the system was built, how it works, and how it makes decisions.

Accountability refers to the ability to hold individuals or organizations responsible for the actions and decisions made by the AGI system. This includes understanding the decision-making process, being able to identify who is responsible for the system's actions, and ensuring that there are mechanisms in place to address any negative consequences or harm caused by the system.

Transparency and accountability are essential to building trust in AGI and ensuring that the system is developed in a way that benefits society as a whole. Without them, there is a risk that the technology could be misused or that unintended consequences could arise, leading to mistrust and skepticism among the public.

THE ROLE OF GOVERNMENTS AND INTERNATIONAL ORGANIZATIONS IN REGULATING AGI DEVELOPMENT

As AGI has the potential to impact many aspects of society, it is important for governments and international organizations to be involved in its regulation and governance. Governments can play a critical role in developing laws and regulations that ensure the safe and ethical development and use of AGI.

International organizations, such as the United Nations, can provide a global platform for coordinating and promoting responsible AGI development. These organizations can facilitate discussions and agreements between nations, establish guidelines and principles for the development and use of AGI, and monitor and enforce compliance with these standards.

Additionally, governments and international organizations can provide funding and support for AGI research and development. This can help ensure that AGI is developed in a way that benefits society as a whole and addresses societal challenges, while also minimizing potential risks and negative impacts.

STAKEHOLDER ENGAGEMENT AND PUBLIC AWARENESS

Stakeholder engagement and public awareness are critical components of AGI governance. The development and deployment of AGI should be done in collaboration with various stakeholders, including scientists, policymakers, business leaders, and the public. The involvement of stakeholders can help ensure that AGI is developed and used in a responsible and ethical manner that benefits society as a whole.

Public awareness is also important in ensuring that the development and deployment of AGI align with societal values and expectations. This can be achieved through public engagement, education, and dialogue on the potential benefits and risks of AGI. Public awareness campaigns can also help address concerns and misconceptions about AGI, promote transparency, and build trust between AGI developers and the public.

Overall, stakeholder engagement and public awareness can help ensure that AGI is developed and deployed in a responsible and ethical manner that benefits society as a whole.

AGI AND SOCIETY

AGI is expected to have a significant impact on society, including various industries and sectors. This chapter explores some of the social and cultural implications of AGI and the need for education and workforce development to keep up with the changes.

One of the potential benefits of AGI is its ability to automate mundane and repetitive tasks, freeing up humans to focus on more complex and creative tasks. This could lead to significant improvements in productivity and efficiency in industries such as manufacturing, transportation, and healthcare.

However, this could also lead to job displacement and the need for workers to develop new skills to keep up with the changing job market. It is essential to invest in education and workforce development programs to help individuals acquire the necessary skills to adapt to the changing job market.

AGI could also have a significant impact on the creative industries, such as music and art, where machines could generate new works and compositions. However, the question of whether these works can be considered authentic or original remains a topic of debate.

Another important consideration is the potential impact of AGI on privacy and security. As machines become more intelligent and capable, they could collect and analyze vast amounts of data, raising concerns about privacy and security. It is important to develop robust security measures and policies to ensure that individuals' data is protected.

Collaboration and partnerships are critical in the development and deployment of AGI. Governments, private companies, and research institutions must work together to ensure that AGI is developed in a way that benefits society as a whole. This includes addressing issues such as ethics, transparency, and accountability.

In summary, the social and cultural implications of AGI are far-reaching, and it is essential to develop education and workforce development programs that can help individuals adapt to the changing job market. It is also crucial to consider the potential impact of AGI on privacy and security and to develop strong policies and regulations to address these issues. Collaboration and partnerships are critical in ensuring that AGI is developed and deployed in a responsible and beneficial way for society.

SOCIAL AND CULTURAL IMPLICATIONS OF AGI

The development of AGI has significant social and cultural implications that need to be carefully considered. One of the main concerns is the potential impact on employment and the labor market. AGI could automate many jobs, leading to job displacement and potentially exacerbating income inequality. This could also have a broader impact on the economy, with many people losing their jobs and requiring support to find new employment.

Another concern is the potential for AGI to widen existing social and cultural divides. For example, if AGI is primarily developed and used by certain groups, it could further exclude or marginalize other groups, exacerbating existing inequalities. Additionally, there is a risk that AGI could perpetuate biases and discrimination that exist in society, particularly if the data used to train AGI models contains biases.

There is also a need to consider the potential impact of AGI on education and knowledge production. AGI could significantly impact how knowledge is created, shared, and utilized, potentially transforming the role of educators, researchers, and scholars. This could have significant implications for education and workforce development, requiring new skills and training for individuals to adapt to the changing landscape.

Finally, AGI also raises ethical and moral questions around the nature of intelligence and consciousness, and how we should treat intelligent machines. These questions have significant implications for society and require careful consideration and discussion to ensure that AGI is developed and deployed in an ethical and responsible manner.

THE IMPACT ON DIFFERENT INDUSTRIES AND SECTORS

The impact of AGI on different industries and sectors is expected to be significant. AGI has the potential to transform various fields, including healthcare, finance, transportation, manufacturing, and entertainment. For instance, AGI can be used in healthcare for disease diagnosis, drug discovery, and personalized medicine. In finance, AGI can help with fraud detection, credit scoring, and investment decision-making. In transportation, AGI can assist with autonomous vehicles and traffic management. In manufacturing, AGI can be used for predictive maintenance, quality control, and supply chain optimization. In entertainment, AGI can be used for personalized content recommendations and creating lifelike characters and scenes.

AGI can also have a significant impact on the labor market. While AGI has the potential to create new job opportunities, it can also lead to job displacement as machines take over tasks that were previously performed by humans. This could lead to significant changes in the way people work and the skills that are required for different jobs. It is therefore essential to consider the impact of AGI on the labor market and ensure that workers are equipped with the necessary skills to adapt to the changing work environment.

EDUCATION AND WORKFORCE DEVELOPMENT

AGI is expected to have a significant impact on the job market and workforce in the coming years. It will create new job opportunities that require new skills and expertise, while also displacing many jobs that are susceptible to automation. As such, it is important to prepare the workforce for this transition and ensure that everyone has the opportunity to acquire the necessary skills and knowledge to succeed in the new job market.

Education and training will play a critical role in ensuring a smooth transition to the age of AGI. There is a need to develop new educational programs and training initiatives that focus on the skills and competencies that will be in demand in the new job market. These may include programming, data analysis, machine learning, and other technical skills, as well as soft skills such as creativity, critical thinking, and problem-solving.

In addition, there is a need to address the digital divide and ensure that everyone has access to the necessary technology and resources to participate in the digital economy. This includes investing in infrastructure, providing access to affordable high-speed internet, and addressing disparities in education and training opportunities.

Governments, educational institutions, and industry leaders will need to work together to develop a comprehensive strategy for education and workforce development in the age of AGI. This will involve collaboration and partnerships across sectors, as well as innovative approaches to training and education that take into account the rapidly changing landscape of the job market.

COLLABORATION AND PARTNERSHIPS

Collaboration and partnerships are crucial for the successful development and deployment of AGI. AGI development involves a diverse set of skills and expertise, including computer science, neuroscience, philosophy, psychology, and more. Therefore, collaboration and partnerships are necessary to bring together experts from different fields to work towards a common goal.

Collaboration and partnerships can also facilitate knowledge sharing and best practices, accelerating the pace of AGI development. Additionally, collaborations with industry, academia, and governments can help identify the most pressing challenges and opportunities, and prioritize research and development efforts accordingly.

Partnerships with businesses can also help drive innovation and commercialization of AGI technology, creating new products and services that can benefit society. Governments can play a crucial role in facilitating collaboration and partnerships, providing funding, resources, and support for AGI research and development.

Overall, collaboration and partnerships can help ensure that AGI development is ethical, responsible, and serves the best interests of society as a whole.

THE FUTURE OF AGI

The development of AGI is still in its early stages, but it has the potential to fundamentally transform society and the world as we know it. In this chapter, we will explore some possible scenarios for the future of AGI and its impact on various aspects of our lives.

One potential scenario is that AGI will lead to significant job displacement and economic disruption, as many tasks currently performed by humans will be automated. This could result in significant social and economic upheaval, and there will be a need for new types of jobs and skills.

Another possible outcome is that AGI will enable the creation of new products and services, leading to economic growth and increased prosperity. This could have a positive impact on society, but there will also be challenges, such as ensuring that the benefits of AGI are distributed fairly across different groups and regions.

AGI could also have a significant impact on the environment. For example, it could enable the development of new technologies to mitigate climate change and reduce our carbon footprint. However, it could also lead to the creation of new types of waste and pollution, and there will be a need to ensure that AGI is developed and deployed in an environmentally sustainable way.

Another important consideration is the role of humans in a world with AGI. It is likely that humans will continue to play an important role in many areas, such as creative endeavors, interpersonal interactions, and decision-making. However, the nature of work and the economy may change significantly, and there will be a need to ensure that humans are able to thrive in a world with AGI.

Overall, the future of AGI is uncertain, and there are many challenges and opportunities ahead. It will be important for governments, international organizations, stakeholders, and the public to work together to ensure that AGI is developed and deployed in a way that maximizes its benefits and minimizes its risks. This will require ongoing dialogue, collaboration, and education, as well as a commitment to transparency and accountability.

SCENARIOS FOR THE FUTURE OF AGI

There are several scenarios for the future of AGI, ranging from highly optimistic to highly pessimistic. Here are some possible scenarios:

Utopian: AGI is developed in a way that benefits all of humanity, solving global problems and making life easier and more enjoyable for everyone.

Dystopian: AGI becomes uncontrollable and dominates humanity, resulting in a world where humans are subservient to machines.

Coexistence: AGI and humans coexist, with AGI serving as a tool to augment human capabilities and enhance our quality of life.

Limited impact: AGI has a limited impact on society, being used mainly in research and development, with few applications in the real world.

Mixed impact: AGI has both positive and negative impacts on society, depending on how it is developed and deployed.

Gradual evolution: AGI develops slowly over time, with incremental improvements leading to significant advances in the long term.

Rapid evolution: AGI develops rapidly, with breakthroughs occurring at an increasingly fast pace, leading to a world where technology advances at an exponential rate.

It is difficult to predict which scenario will come to pass, as it depends on how AGI is developed, deployed, and regulated in the coming years.

THE IMPACT OF AGI ON THE ECONOMY, SOCIETY, AND THE ENVIRONMENT

The impact of AGI on the economy, society, and the environment is likely to be significant. In terms of the economy, AGI has the potential to revolutionize industries and create new ones, leading to job creation and increased productivity. However, there are also concerns about job displacement and economic disruption, particularly in sectors that are heavily reliant on manual labor.

In terms of society, AGI could bring about significant improvements in areas such as healthcare, education, and public safety. For example, AGI-powered healthcare systems could enable more accurate diagnoses and personalized treatments, while AGI-powered education systems could offer personalized learning experiences and reduce educational inequalities. However, there are also concerns about the ethical and social implications of AGI, including issues around privacy, bias, and the concentration of power.

In terms of the environment, AGI could play a significant role in addressing some of the world's most pressing environmental challenges, such as climate change and resource depletion. For example, AGI-powered technologies could enable more efficient use of resources and more accurate climate modeling. However, there are also concerns that AGI could exacerbate environmental issues if it is not developed and deployed responsibly.

Overall, the impact of AGI on the economy, society, and the environment is likely to be complex and multifaceted, with both opportunities and challenges. It will be important for developers, policymakers, and other stakeholders to consider these issues carefully as they work to create a future that maximizes the benefits of AGI while minimizing its risks.

THE ROLE OF HUMANS IN A WORLD WITH AGI

As AGI continues to develop, there is much debate about the role of humans in a world with AGI. Some experts believe that AGI could lead to job displacement, while others believe that it could lead to new job opportunities and a more productive workforce.

In a world with AGI, humans would need to adapt to working alongside intelligent machines, and there may be a shift towards more creative and innovative jobs that require human intuition and decision-making. Humans may also need to take on more supervisory roles, overseeing the work of intelligent machines and ensuring that they are operating safely and ethically.

There are also concerns about the impact of AGI on human identity and culture. As intelligent machines become more advanced and capable of performing tasks traditionally done by humans, there may be a shift in the way we define ourselves and our place in society. Additionally, the widespread use of AGI could lead to a loss of privacy and autonomy, as machines become more involved in every aspect of our lives.

Overall, the role of humans in a world with AGI is still uncertain, but it is clear that there will be significant changes and challenges ahead. It will be important for society to address these challenges proactively and work towards a future where humans and machines can coexist and thrive together.

THE CHALLENGES AND OPPORTUNITIES AHEAD

As AGI continues to advance and become more integrated into our daily lives, it presents both challenges and opportunities. One of the main challenges is ensuring that AGI is developed and deployed in an ethical and responsible manner, with proper consideration given to potential risks and unintended consequences. This requires collaboration and partnerships between stakeholders, including governments, international organizations, industry leaders, researchers, and the public.

Another challenge is ensuring that the benefits of AGI are distributed fairly and equitably, without exacerbating existing inequalities or creating new ones. This requires careful consideration of education and workforce development, as well as policies and regulations that promote access and opportunity for all.

Despite these challenges, the opportunities presented by AGI are vast. AGI has the potential to transform many industries and sectors, from healthcare and transportation to finance and manufacturing. It can help us solve some of the world's most pressing problems, such as climate change, poverty, and disease.

Moreover, AGI has the potential to enhance human capabilities and lead to a more collaborative and connected society. It can also free us from mundane and repetitive tasks, allowing us to focus on more creative and fulfilling endeavors.

In conclusion, the future of AGI is full of possibilities and potential, but it requires careful consideration of the ethical, social, and environmental implications. By working together, we can ensure that AGI is developed and deployed in a responsible and beneficial way, creating a better future for all.

CONCLUSION

The conclusion chapter serves as a summary of the main ideas discussed throughout the book, highlighting the potential benefits and risks of AGI. It emphasizes the importance of considering the ethical and societal implications of AGI development and deployment, and the need for collaboration and partnerships among various stakeholders.

The chapter also explores the implications for the future of AGI, discussing potential scenarios and their impact on the economy, society, and the environment. It suggests that AGI has the potential to revolutionize many industries and fields, but also poses significant challenges and risks that must be addressed.

Finally, the chapter provides recommendations for future research and policy development in the field of AGI, emphasizing the need for interdisciplinary collaboration, transparency, and accountability. It suggests that ethical considerations and stakeholder engagement should be at the forefront of AGI development and deployment, and that policymakers and regulators should play a key role in ensuring that AGI is developed and deployed in a responsible and beneficial manner.

SUMMARY OF THE KEY POINTS
MADE IN THE BOOK

This book provides an in-depth exploration of artificial general intelligence (AGI), its current state of development, and its potential benefits and risks. Here are the key points made in the book:

● AGI is a type of AI that can perform any intellectual task that a human can.

● AGI has the potential to revolutionize numerous fields, from healthcare to transportation, and to solve some of the world's most pressing problems, including climate change and global poverty.

● There are numerous challenges to developing AGI, including the lack of understanding of human cognition and the limitations of current computing technology.

● AGI also presents significant risks, including job displacement, existential risks, bias, and ethical considerations.

● To mitigate these risks, transparency, accountability, and ethical considerations are critical in the development and deployment of AGI.

● Collaboration and partnerships are also necessary among various stakeholders, including governments, international organizations, industry, academia, and the public.

● The future of AGI is uncertain, but it has the potential to significantly impact the economy, society, and the environment, and the role of humans in a world with AGI is still unclear.

● Further research and policy development are necessary to ensure the safe and beneficial development of AGI.

Overall, the book highlights the immense potential and significant risks of AGI, and the importance of responsible development and deployment to ensure its safe and beneficial use for humanity.

IMPLICATIONS FOR THE FUTURE OF AGI AND ITS IMPACT ON SOCIETY

The implications for the future of AGI are vast and could have significant impacts on society, the economy, and the environment. With the potential to solve complex problems and improve decision-making, AGI has the potential to transform many industries and sectors. However, it also poses risks and unintended consequences, including job displacement, ethical considerations, and potential existential risks.

To mitigate these risks and maximize the benefits, there is a need for collaboration and partnerships among stakeholders, including governments, international organizations, and the public. Additionally, there is a need for transparency and accountability in AGI development, as well as education and workforce development to prepare for a world with AGI.

The impact of AGI on society will depend on how it is developed and deployed. It has the potential to improve healthcare, education, and transportation, among other areas. However, it also poses challenges for privacy, security, and ethics. The role of humans in a world with AGI remains uncertain, and there is a need to consider how humans can work alongside AGI and maintain control and agency.

Overall, the future of AGI is promising but also poses challenges and risks that need to be addressed through collaborative efforts and responsible governance.

RECOMMENDATIONS FOR FUTURE RESEARCH AND POLICY DEVELOPMENT

Here are some potential recommendations for future research and policy development related to AGI:

Foster interdisciplinary collaborations: AGI research requires a multidisciplinary approach, including expertise in computer science, cognitive science, neuroscience, philosophy, ethics, and social sciences. Encouraging collaboration across these fields can help address the complex challenges of AGI.

Develop transparent and ethical guidelines: To ensure the safe and responsible development of AGI, guidelines and ethical standards should be established and enforced. These guidelines should be transparent, publicly accessible, and regularly updated to keep up with technological advancements.

Address potential biases and unintended consequences: AGI developers and policymakers should be aware of the potential biases and unintended consequences of AGI and take steps to address them. This includes ensuring that AGI is developed with diversity and inclusivity in mind.

Promote education and workforce development: The development of AGI will require a workforce with a unique set of skills, including expertise in AI, data science, and machine learning. Promoting education and workforce development in these areas can help prepare individuals for the jobs of the future.

Encourage public dialogue and engagement: As AGI technology continues to advance, it is important to engage with the public and encourage a dialogue about its potential benefits and risks.

This includes addressing concerns about job displacement and existential risks.

Foster international collaboration: The development of AGI is a global endeavor, and international collaboration can help ensure that the technology is developed in a safe, responsible, and ethical manner.

Develop robust safety mechanisms: AGI technology is inherently unpredictable, and safety mechanisms must be in place to prevent catastrophic outcomes. Research should focus on developing these safety mechanisms, including fail-safe mechanisms and human-AI collaboration.

ABOUT THE AUTHOR

Krikor Karaoghlanian

Krikor Karaoghlanian is a digital printing expert and logo designer with over a decade of experience in the printing industry. He is also a passionate writer and has recently taken up writing books as a new hobby, using AI language models such as ChatGPT.

BOOKS BY THIS AUTHOR

Robotions: The Emotions Of Robots: The Rise Of Emotional Intelligence In Robots

This book provides an overview of robotics, covering topics such as emotional AI, robot locomotion and mobility, robot perception and sensing, robot control and actuation, robot applications and industries, and ethics and social implications of robotics.

The book starts by discussing the emergence of emotional AI, the theories of emotion, and the current state of emotional AI research, as well as the applications and ethical considerations. The following chapters cover the types of robots, their components, and the advantages and disadvantages of using robotics. The book also provides an in-depth analysis of robot locomotion and mobility, including the types of robot locomotion, robot mobility systems, kinematics, and motion planning.

In addition, the book covers the sensing and perception aspects of robotics, including the sensor technologies used, vision and image processing, object recognition and localization, and machine perception and learning. The control and actuation chapter covers control systems and techniques, robot actuators and manipulators, robot motion control, and robot grippers and end effectors.

The book then examines the various applications of robotics in different industries, including manufacturing and automation, healthcare, agriculture, construction, and space exploration. The final chapters address the ethical and social implications of robotics, including ethical issues, social and economic impact, robotic laws and regulations, and the future of robotics and society.

Overall, this book provides a comprehensive overview of robotics, highlighting its technological advancements and its impact on society.

Hu-Ai: Switching Between Human And Ai: Exploring A World Where Humans And Machines Trade Places

In "Hu-AI: Switching Between Human and AI," we explore a fascinating world where humans and machines trade places, blurring the boundaries between human and machine. Through the lens of the "switch," we will uncover the implications of this technology on society and on our own sense of self. We will examine the possibilities and challenges of this technology, and the impact it may have on the way we live, work, and relate to each other. Join us on this mind-bending journey of discovery, as we explore the brave new world of human-machine interaction.

Gnikniht: Thinking Backwards

"GNIKNIHT: Thinking Backwards" is a book that explores the concept of reverse thinking and its potential to transform the way we approach problems and make decisions. Through an exploration of the benefits and challenges of reverse thinking, the book offers practical tools and insights for individuals and organizations looking to embrace this innovative approach to problem-solving.

The book covers a range of topics related to reverse

thinking, including cultivating a reverse thinking mindset, overcoming mental blocks, harnessing creativity, and applying reverse thinking to various aspects of life, including personal relationships, business, and decision-making. Throughout the book, readers will find real-life examples of individuals and organizations that have successfully applied reverse thinking to achieve remarkable success.

Whether you're a business leader, an entrepreneur, or simply an individual looking for fresh ways to approach life's challenges, "GNIKNIHT: Thinking Backwards" offers a powerful framework for unlocking your full potential and achieving success through reverse thinking.

Yenom Venom: Exploring The Dark Side Of Money

In "YENOM VENOM: Exploring the Dark Side of Money," AI writer expert Krikor Karaoghlanian takes readers on a journey to explore the complex world of money and its impact on our lives. Through a series of thought-provoking chapters, Krikor delves into the history of money, the psychological and emotional impact of money, and the dark side of wealth and debt. He then offers a practical framework for reframing our thinking and setting meaningful goals that align with our values, ultimately helping us cultivate a healthier relationship with money and live a more fulfilling life. This book is a must-read for anyone seeking to break free from the negative cycle of money and achieve financial and personal success.

Reboot: Rethinking Humanity In The Age Of Ai: How To Embrace The Future By Rebooting Your Mind

"Reboot: Rethinking Humanity in the Age of AI" is a thought-provoking book that explores the impact of artificial intelligence and robotics on various aspects of human life, including communication, relationships, the workplace, social interactions, and personal and family life. The book emphasizes the need for a human-centered approach to technology design and development, and provides practical guidance on implementing human-centered design principles. Through a growth mindset and collaborative approach, readers can learn to embrace the future and build a more human-centered society that integrates technology in a responsible and ethical manner."

Ai Messages To Humanity

"AI Messages to Humanity" is a thought-provoking and insightful book that explores the role of artificial intelligence in our society. Through a series of 66 messages divided into three volumes, the book offers a unique perspective on the benefits and risks of AI, as well as the ethical considerations and responsibilities of those who develop and use it. Each message is accompanied by a beautiful and inspiring AI-generated image that enhances the reader's experience. This book is perfect for anyone interested in philosophy, technology, and the intersection between the two."

Ai Jokes: 75 Hilarious Jokes From The World Of Ai

Looking for a good laugh? Look no further than "Ai Jokes - 75 Hilarious Jokes from the World of AI"! This collection of one-liners and witty observations is guaranteed to tickle your funny bone and leave you in stitches.

With 75 jokes to choose from, you'll be sure to find something to suit your sense of humor. Whether you're a tech enthusiast or just looking for a good joke, "Ai Jokes" is the perfect book to brighten up your day.

So why wait? Order your copy of "Ai Jokes - 75 Hilarious Jokes from the World of AI" today and start laughing your way through the world of artificial intelligence! And remember, as the AI might say, "Why did the computer go to the doctor? Because it had a virus!"

"Special thanks to ChatGPT, the AI language model that contributed to the creation of the jokes in this book. Its creativity and humor added a unique twist to the world of AI comedy."

Robance: Love In The Age Of Machines

"Robance: Love in the Age of Machines" is a captivating novel that explores the complexities of love in a world where technology has become all-encompassing. X1 and Y1's love story is unconventional, facing challenges and obstacles that put their relationship to the test. As they navigate their way through societal pressures, personal sacrifices, and emotional turmoil, X1 and Y1 learn the true meaning of love and its power to overcome all barriers. This thought-provoking novel offers a poignant reflection on the human experience, reminding us that love is an enduring force that prevails, even in the age of machines.

Six-Sixty-Six: Can You Unlock The Hidden Message?

Welcome to "Six Sixty-Six," an interactive game that will test your skills and challenge your mind.
The game consists of 66 words, each with exactly 6 letters.
But there's more to this game than meets the eye.
Can you uncover the hidden message by finding some of the first letter of each word?
It won't be easy.
You'll need a pen and paper
Dive in and start playing! See if you can unravel the mystery behind "Six Sixty-Six."

Order 'Six Sixty-Six' today!

Your Brain Your Prison: Within Yourself

Discover the invisible prison within your own mind with "Your Brain Your Prison: Within Yourself." This thought-provoking book delves into the ways we can become trapped by our own thoughts, beliefs, and perceptions, and offers practical tips for breaking free.

Written for anyone seeking to understand and overcome self-imposed limitations, this book challenges readers to examine their own mental processes and question the assumptions that hold them back. With insights from psychology, neuroscience, and mindfulness practices, "Your Brain Your Prison: Within Yourself" provides a comprehensive guide to freeing yourself from the confines of your own mind.

Whether you're struggling with self-doubt, anxiety, or just feel stuck in your current circumstances, this book offers a roadmap to greater self-awareness and a more fulfilling life. Join the journey of self-discovery and learn how to break free from the invisible prison of your own mind.

Pizzai: America's Best Pizza, Ai-Approved

Introducing PizzAI: America's Best Pizzas, AI-Approved. cookbook! This must-have cookbook features three of the most beloved pizza styles from across the country, including New York-style, Chicago-style California-style, and California-style. With easy-to-follow recipes and step-by-step instructions, even novice chefs can create delicious and authentic pizza at home. Each recipe includes a carefully curated list of ingredients, guaranteed to elevate your pizza-making game.

Ailiens: When Artificial Intelligence Meets

Extraterrestrial Life: A Science Fiction Tale Of Humanity's Encounter With The Unknown

AILIENS is a thought-provoking science fiction tale about humanity's encounter with the unknown. When a team of scientists discovers an extraterrestrial civilization, they soon realize that their society is built upon advanced artificial intelligence. As they work to bridge the gap between their two worlds and build a shared identity, they must also confront the challenges of integrating vastly different cultures and values.

Written by Krikor Karaoghlanian and ChatGPT, AILIENS combines action, suspense, and philosophy to explore the complexities of human nature and the potential for technology to shape our future. This book is perfect for fans of science fiction who love to explore the mysteries of the universe and ponder the possibilities of what lies beyond.

Read This Now!: 50 Quotes Power

"Read This Now!: 50 Quotes Power" is a book that contains 50 powerful and inspirational quotes that will motivate and empower readers to live their best lives. Each quote is carefully selected to provide a unique perspective on life, love, success, and happiness. With stunning visuals generated by Midjourney, this book is a perfect addition to any coffee table or bookshelf. Whether you need a quick pick-me-up or a daily dose of inspiration, "Read This Now!: 50 Quotes Power" is a must-read for anyone seeking to live a fulfilling life.